How To Become A Successful Bodyguard

Published By Shaharm Publications

SHAHARM PUBLICATIONS

For a full list of books by Shaharm Publications, please go to:

http://www.shaharmpublications.com

TABLE OF CONTENTS

SO YOU WANT TO BE A BODYGUARD

A lot of people think that becoming a bodyguard would be a lot of fun. They believe that bodyguards lead exciting lives and that the job is one that anyone who is tough, strong or otherwise physically intimidating could do well at. The truth is that becoming a successful bodyguard requires more than martial arts skills and an imposing presence. The job of a bodyguard is one that includes a lot of research, planning and negotiation.

Bodyguards must be proficient in not just dealing with physical threats when they do occur, but also in preventing the threats from surfacing in the first place. This can sometimes mean trying to tactfully change the way that the client behaves. If a client really is in danger, then they will need to think carefully about where they go and who they spend time with. This is something that they might not appreciate.

It is difficult to change the behavior of someone who has spent many years doing their own thing, but a good bodyguard can explain the reasons why this is important, and can act to improve the safety of a person at home, at work, and when they are travelling. Let's take a look at the responsibilities of a bodyguard, and what each part of their job entails. Are you up to the task?

WHAT DOES A BODYGUARD DO?

A bodyguard is responsible for the personal security of their customers. They will usually work as a part of a team, with a personal bodyguard providing a visible deterrent and helping to keep minor threats (such as over-enthusiastic fans, in the case of a celebrity) out of the way. The bodyguard will probably have a team of security officers working with them to secure the residence and any places where the client is making an appearance.

It is important to note that bodyguards do far more than just react to threats, they also:

- Assess potential threats and work to prevent them.

- Take care of security at home, in the office, at public venues and in other areas where the client maybe spending time.

- Search and assess areas before the client enters them.

- Ensure the security of the customer when they are travelling

- Ensure the security of any vehicles used or boarded by the customer.

- Perform reconnaissance of commonly travelled routes, and prepare travel plans to protect against ambush or attack.

- Teach the customer basic personal awareness and safety skills if they are receptive to this.

- Are trained in the operation of legal weapons.

- Are trained in unarmed combat.

- Know how to de-escalate situations, and when the use of weapons or force is necessary.

- Are trained in life-saving first-aid techniques.

The world of Close Protection and bodyguard work has changed a lot in recent years, and in most parts of the world the industry is now far better regulated than ever before. This is good news for those who are seeking protection, and it serves to weed out those who believe that close protection is an easy job, but it does mean that it can be intimidating getting started in the industry. The number of identity checks, criminal record checks and training policies that are required for someone looking to get started in the industry is potentially daunting.

Even after that baseline of qualifications has been established, it is important that you understand exactly what your job entails. Experience working as a doorman or a general security guard is a good starting point, and experience working as a police officer or time in a specialist military organization will also serve as a good starting point, but beyond that the only way to become a successful bodyguard is to spend time shadowing other bodyguards or working as a part of a team until you understand each part of the job.

The most successful bodyguards address threats before they become serious. In many countries, the person to be protected by a bodyguard is called a principal. The principal and the customer may not always be the same person. There are several standards and rules of operation that a bodyguard should follow, and an order in which they should follow them. Typically, a bodyguard will:

- Assess the level of threat that the principal faces and identify key risk areas.

- Plan out ways to minimize those threats and prepare risk-reduction measures to protect the principal.

- Liaise with the principal and any key persons who will be involved in those plans.

- Create secure environments for the principal and ensure that they are properly maintained.

- Communicate with the principal and other key persons while engaged in their protection.

- Ensure that the principal is protected both on-foot and while in a vehicle.

- Respond to potential conflicts through threat management and de-escalation where possible, and control or restraint when necessary.

- Respond quickly and effectively to any medical crises or trauma faced by the principal.

Failure in any one of those areas could cause serious problems for the principal, and lead to them coming to harm. A bodyguard must always be alert and must follow the correct procedures at all times, while relying on their backup team to also do the same. This requires several competencies, which are outlined below.

IMPROVING PERSONAL SECURITY

One of the core competencies that any bodyguard will have is the ability to maintain the safety and personal security of their principal or principals while they are out and about in public, especially while on foot. To do this, they must maintain effective communication both with the principal themselves and with any members of your team. Your principal must understand the importance of following any commands or signals that you give them, should a threat arise.

When most people think of bodyguards, they think of big men in suits, wearing earpieces, that follow celebrities around. While you will spend some time as a bodyguard walking alongside the principal, this is not the only part of your job. The bodyguard that is visible, and close to the principal, is acting partly as a buffer against personal contact and partly as a deterrent. The visible bodyguard is also expected to be watching those around the principal, being aware of instances where the principal is under surveillance, or otherwise being intruded upon.

The bodyguard's primary responsibility is to protect the health and safety of the principal. This may require taking into account any medical conditions or mobility issues the principal has. For example, if a diabetic is detained somewhere, they may be under threat simply from loss of access to their medication. A good bodyguard will be aware of this and will monitor the principal's health and wellbeing, taking this threat as seriously as any other that they face.

Communication is Key

While you are escorting your principal on foot you must communicate with them clearly, and make sure that they

8

understand any signals that you plan to use. Some principals may resent having a visible escort, and in those cases you must work to get them on your side and to understand the importance of the work that you are doing before you head out in public with them.

Try to reach an agreement about the level of protection that they are given. If they do not want a full team of bodyguards walking alongside them, can you reduce the visible presence without reducing their personal security? Having some bodyguards follow at a discrete distance could make the principal feel more comfortable without sacrificing the quality of the protection too much. A principal that is happy to work with you is safer than one that resents your presence.

While on foot, a principal can face several forms of attack, ranging from verbal harassment to having objects thrown at them, attack from hysterical crowds, shooting with a firearm, physical attack either from an unarmed assailant or a weapon, or more extreme methods such as bombing or arson. As a bodyguard it is your job to be aware of these threats and to have a clear escape plan.

There are many things that could hinder your escape, including blocked doors, broken escalators or lifts, corridors that become congested through crowding, or even simply surfaces that are difficult to navigate at speed in inappropriate footwear. Corners, dark areas and exposed plazas can be a threat in many cases too, especially if the principal is someone who has had threats on their life and requires the highest form of security.

To offer the best service to the principal, a bodyguard should get to know the typical behavior patterns of the person that they are working with. Their mannerisms and temperament can influence the way that you should treat them and work with them. Depending on the law in the area you are operating, you may find that there are limits to the kind of protection that you can offer, and you should consider those limitations when building your personal security plan.

If your principal has been threatened, or has had security issues in the past, then this is something that you should pay close attention to. Any existing threats can be used to inform the protection plans that you come up with. However, it is important that you do not obsess over those threats to the point of ignoring other threats. The entire bodyguard team should be on the lookout for potential fresh threats at all times.

When it comes to personal security, the role of the bodyguard begins before you even step outside of the house. The bodyguard should assess any potential threats via some preliminary research, and then select a route that will offer a safe, smooth and efficient pathway for the principal from their starting point to their destination. They should perform reconnaissance on that route, then escort the principal along it, using a team of people to provide protection if necessary.

The problem that bodyguards often face is having to explain to a principal that short detours or sudden changes in destination are not a good idea. The principal may express a desire to stop off along the way, or head to somewhere not in the plan. Adapting to those changes is sometimes possible, but it should only be done if the safety of the principal will not be compromised in any way.

In busy cities and crowded areas, monitoring those around the principal to identify anyone who may be observing the principal or planning an attack can be difficult. If the principal is a public figure then telling the difference between a well-meaning fan and a potential threat is going to be a hard task, and a task that will crop up often. It is important that you have good conflict management skills and are able to make decisions quickly based on limited information.

Bodyguards will have to handle a lot of incidents during their careers, and will also face many dilemmas. Is that person approaching the principal dangerous? Is the fire alarm going off in this shopping area because of a random incident, or an attempt to deal harm to the principal? Which exit is the safest one to take in this incident?

A bodyguard must be able to assess the information that is available to them right now, identify the potential courses of action, weigh the benefits and downsides of each, and then take action in a confident and assertive fashion, ensuring the compliance of the principal. If the principal panics or is hurt then they must be given assistance to ensure that they make it out safely.

Security will always, to some extent, require compromises. Unless the principal is locked away in a "panic room" with multiple redundant security systems there will always be some way that a person could get access to them to do them harm. Bodyguards must decide the right balance between offering protection to a principal while not using excessive manpower and while not restricting the freedom and privacy of the principal any more than necessary.

The problem with these compromises is that as the teams get smaller and the principal (as well as his or her non-security trained entourage) has more authority, the risk to the principal becomes greater. If a VIP is being taken to a concert and a traffic incident causes them to be separated from the convoy of security vehicles travelling with them, should the VIP keep going, or wait to allows the convoy to catch up? If the principal is approached by a fan, how much contact should the fan have with the principal?

Personal security covers all of these issues. A good bodyguard will have rehearsed how to handle the kinds of incidents that are likely to occur when escorting someone. Many military and law enforcement organizations that offer training for bodyguards use reactionary drills which can help to prepare people for such situations.

The Weakness of Reactionary Drills

Unfortunately, reactionary drills alone are not enough to ensure that the plans you create will be executed effectively under pressure. When it comes to incident management, the only way to really ensure that the correct response will be initiated instinctively and promptly is to practice that response repeatedly under pressure. Some reactionary drills do encourage this, but some have a built-in cognitive element, and this is what makes them ineffective.

Incident response should be drilled in the way that the incident would be handled in real life. This means that it should be done quickly and that the response should be instinctive. There is no time to stop, think, debate or explain when handling a serious incident. Both you and your team should understand this and as far as possible the principal should be "trained" too.

Dilemmas can have a slightly different approach, however. When you are faced with a dilemma you should follow a multi-step process. Firstly, ensure that the principal is not under an immediate threat. Once this is established, take measures to protect the principal's safety in the short therm. Finally, assess the situation and consider options for resolving the dilemma. If the principal cannot travel a certain way because the road is blocked, or they go to check in to a hotel room and the hotel is full, find an alternative route or source of accommodation.

Dilemmas are still a threat to the principal's personal safety, but the threat is not immediate. You have time to consider the situation and assess the value of different options and you should take as much time as you need to weigh the information that is available to you and make a good decision.

Sometimes, this may put you in a position where the principal feels inconvenienced or like their personal privacy is being compromised. The more contingency plans you make the easier it will be for you to keep the principal happy and not interfere with their day-to-day routine. Any dilemmas caused by your own behavior should be taken incredibly seriously both as a customer service issue and as a personal security issue.

YOUR CLIENT'S RESPONSIBILITIES

Your principal is the single most important person that you will be dealing with on a day-to-day basis. The principal could be anyone from an everyday person needing protection in the run-up to a court case to a celebrity or even a child who has had a bodyguard hired for them by a parent who is concerned that the child is in danger from the other parent. Some people are grateful for the protection that a bodyguard offers, others are resentful of their presence.

The principal should, in theory, be allowed to move freely. It is your job to ensure that they are offered the best protection possible. Ideally, you should allow the principal to continue their day-to-day routine while still protecting them. Some principals – especially politicians and company leaders – may want to present the image of someone who needs minimal security and may prefer their bodyguards to be as discreet as possible.

Working to protect themselves

Wherever possible, the bodyguard should discuss the principal's day-to-day routine with them and learn as much as they can about their habits and preferences. Any core security issues should be discussed in advance, and the principal should be given an explanation of the signals and orders that the bodyguard wishes to use in their day-to-day work.

The bodyguard may want to explain some basic personal security habits to the principal. Many people are unaware of basic awareness, de-escalation and observation techniques, as well as threat assessment skills that could save their lives. Engaging the principal for long enough to explain these things could be an issue, but it is something that the bodyguard should try to do.

Security begins with small changes such as making sure that downstairs windows are locked, checking the peephole before answering the door, always engaging the car alarm before walking away, and trying to avoid being out late at night unaccompanied. These may all sound like common sense, but if someone has been habitually breaking any of those rules, getting them to put their personal safety first may be a challenge.

It is important that the principal understands three important rules – firstly, to a large extent, they are responsible for their own security. The bodyguard can only do so much, and if the principal acts in a way that prevents the bodyguard from doing their job, then any risk they face is their own fault.

Secondly, the security measures that are taken by the bodyguard and their team should reflect the level of the threat that is being posed. Excessive security measures are expensive, restrictive and invasive. It is better to practice reasonable precautions, and allow the principal to retain as much freedom as possible.

Thirdly, both the principal and the bodyguard should practice mindfulness and awareness. Simply paying attention to your surroundings is a good starting point for identifying and avoiding threats, and preventing potentially dangerous situations from escalating.

A principal that understands that they are responsible for their own personal security is one of the best kinds of person to work with. They are more likely to appreciate rules number two and three and to make an effort to be reasonable in their requests, and to be aware of their surroundings. However, being constantly aware of what is going on around you is exceedingly tiring – even professionals make mistakes sometimes.

Awareness is one area where people slip up on a regular basis. When in a new environment, people suffer from information overload and fatigue incredibly quickly. When in a familiar environment, people fall back on old habitual behaviors and their ability to process new or unexpected information fatigues. Your conscious mind can only hold on to a thought for a few seconds at a time, and when distractions appear any plans to stay alert will vanish.

Awareness, on a long-term level, is something that must be trained. Law enforcement officers and people in the military drill threat awareness and evaluation on a regular basis and hone their observation skills over a long period of time. You can teach this skill to your principals, if they are willing to practice it, but you cannot expect them to become proficient in a short period of time.

When dealing with threats, the most important thing is to focus on threat awareness. After a threat is identified, it must be evaluated. Following threat evaluation the next challenge is to find a way to avoid the threat.

Ideally, threats should be noticed well in advance of them becoming a problem. If a threat is not spotted until the last possible moment, then there will not be enough time to evaluate it and enact an avoidance plan.

While you are with your principal, you will likely be focusing on threat awareness and personal safety for them, but you can still teach them to identify hazards for themselves. For example, you should educate them about strategies such as walking facing oncoming traffic, and not wearing earphones while they are walking alone late at night – so that they can hear people following them.

The sooner someone is aware that they are being followed, or notices that they are being approached by, or watched by, someone who appears aggressive or intoxicated, the longer they will have to think about whether the person is a threat. Once they have decided whether they feel they are in danger they can then take action to avoid that person or otherwise protect themselves.

Condition Red?

Many close protection firms use a series of "condition" color codes to identify awareness threats. The first condition is white. White means completely unaware. People who are in "condition white" are not bothered about looking for threats, and they are both mentally and physically unprepared for one to happen. This is not a condition that someone who is working with a bodyguard should be spending time in. If someone's safety has ever been threatened, they should work to be mindful of their surroundings at all time.

Condition yellow is a slightly more heightened state of alertness. This is the ideal condition for someone who has some concerns about their safety. While they may not be pre-occupied with looking for threats at all times, they are at least aware that there could be something going on. It is relatively easy for someone who is well trained to put themselves in this condition, but it is harder for someone who is untrained to stay there.

A bodyguard that is invested in the safety of their principals will work to educate the principal and help them to build the habits that will allow them to maintain that state of awareness. It is the principal's responsibility to work on their development and to build habits that will serve them well after the protection duty is done.

Condition orange – this is a state in which the observer has identified that there could be a threat. They have some time (sometimes minutes, but often only seconds) to assess that threat and decide what kind of action to take. For a bodyguard, this is where their training and drilling will come in. For the principal, this is the opportunity for them to evaluate the threat and take evasive action.

Condition red is the point that no one wants to spend time in, because this mean that they have seen a threat and now no longer have the option of decision-making – action is mandated. By this point the only two actions that are feasible are likely fight or flight. Someone who had spotted a threat earlier may have had more actions open to them.

Fighting is rarely an option

Your principal may ask you to teach them how to fight. When they are told that body guarding is not all about hand-to-hand combat they may respond with disappointment or anger. Most people, even those who are fit and well educated, still carry a lot of misconceptions about fighting and about martial arts.

It is common for people to buy in to the idea that there are secret techniques that can be used to disarm or disable attackers. The idea that fighting requires fitness, timing and practice as well as toughness is hard to accept. It is even harder to accept that fighting is messy and that sometimes even the most highly trained person can be injured by someone less experienced. Removing the impression of fighting as a safe and simple thing is essential.

If your principal insists on learning to defend themselves, then the best option is to show them how to break away from an assailant, create space, and flee. Teaching anything else would be irresponsible and may give them an unrealistic idea of how to deal with an attacker.

Learning basic de-escalation and escape techniques will help the principal with a lot of situations, and will make it easier for you to do your job as a bodyguard. If the prevention of kidnapping is one of the things that you are concerned with, then you as a bodyguard may have the option of working with the principal to educate them on awareness o common techniques. However, you will still need the correct internal expertise, and manpower.

When you first meet your principal, you should run an educational briefing, and discuss with them the risks that they feel that they face, as well as any risks that you have identified. Often, there is less overlap between these things than you might expect. Those who are not experienced in the world of personal protection are likely to overestimate danger in some areas and feel secure in others through complacency or lack of familiarity.

A successful bodyguard will help the principal to get a balanced idea of the risks that they face, and will ensure that they protect themselves in a way that is sufficient, appropriate, and reasonable. Some principals may refuse to accept that risks exist in certain areas and insist on putting themselves in harm's way. Others may physically withdraw from the world to the extreme even though the threats that they face do not warrant it. It is your job to find a realistic and reasonable compromise between those two actions.

One way to help principals understand the risks that they face is to run through the threats with them. A kidnapping or an assassination attempt is highly unlikely to happen out of the blue. There will likely be a long period of surveillance embarked upon first. In addition, such threats occur only where there is a motive. You should discuss this with the principal and reassure them of the research that you have done.

Terrorism is something that some principals may be scared of, and this fear may or may not be a reasonable one. You must always treat the principal as if their fears are reasonable. Explain to them that terrorists usually look for easy targets, and that if you can improve their security to a reasonable degree then they are unlikely to be a target – unless, of course, they are in a position of authority or prominently in the public eye.

Executives and wealthy targets that are concerned about threats on their personal safety, or the safety of their loved ones, being made for the purposes of extorting money, should have plans for the protection of both themselves and the people around them. They should pay particular attention to their safety at home, work, and in social situations in areas where they could be observed to have a routine.

Protecting Information

In today's world of social media, it is easy to find out about the habits and preferences of almost anyone. It is important that the principal and the people around him or her are taught the importance of privacy. They must learn to be mindful when sharing information and to not post anything publically if they do not want people outside of their immediate circle of friends or colleagues to know it.

The principal should not make details of his travel plans available to anyone except those who need to know them, and information such as the layout of the principal's home should not be shared online. Photography should be limited in the home and office, and use of social media platforms such as Facebook and Twitter, while not prohibited, should be carried out with caution.

Most people are creatures of habit, and this makes it easy for an attacker that has been observing the principal and his family to plan their activities. After a few weeks of observation it is likely that the principal will have exhibited an obvious pattern such as leaving for the office at 8AM, picking up a coffee from a specific store at 8:30, and then arriving at the office at 8:45. His wife may visit the same stores every day, and his children may leave school and head to the mall for one hour before returning home.

This information makes it easy to plan kidnapping attempts or to find a time when the home will be empty so that they can break in. While it is not reasonable to expect people to live unpredictable lives every day, there are things that the principal and his family can do to limit the risk they face because of those patterns.

Signs of surveillance include the obvious – such as a vehicle passing by the house slowly several times per day, or spending a lot of time parked by the home. They may be slightly less obvious – such as repair crews spending a lot of time nearby (by the time it is noticed that the repair crew seems to be achieving very little, they may have completed a lot of surveillance), repeated calls from salesmen or religious evangelists, or even the presence of "families" playing outside.

An untrained person may find it difficult to assess whether or not the people they are seeing are really observing them, or whether their presence is entirely co-incidental. However, because they are the one person that spends the most time around their family and in the places where they work and socialize, they are the best qualified to monitor the situation.

The principal should be trained to write down any concerns that they have – if they think that they are being observed, they should not the registration numbers of any vehicles they see, as well as a brief description. If they think they recognize a person that is loitering nearby, note down the time they were seen, and their appearance. If a person is seen walking hand in hand with one "spouse" one day, then is playing the part of a member of another happy couple the following day this is cause for suspicion.

Tell the principal to inform you if they have any concerns, and if that they should not hesitate to contact the police either. It is better to have the police look into any suspicious behavior rather than allow a more serious threat to develop. The principal should educate any people that spend a lot of time with them to follow the same observational behaviors.

If you spend a lot of time with the principal, you can help them to develop this skill by discussing things with them throughout the day. Over time, they will learn what sorts of things you are paying attention to.

Your principal can also practice some small lifestyle changes that will make it harder for people to observer them. For example, if they have the option of using company cars, they could try to drive different ones from time to time, so that the observers can't simply track the movements of one vehicle.

If the principal needs to travel on foot, encourage them to walk with a group of people, and to try to avoid being out late after dark. When socializing, they should try to change the venues they visit on a regular basis. It is not a good idea to be in the habit of using a "local" if you are a public figure.

The principal should keep the police informed about any recent threats, and any planned public appearances. Friends, family members and trustworthy employees should also be kept informed of any potential threats. Those people should be told that they should not share information about the whereabouts of (or personal details of) themselves, their family, or any key personnel with anyone without permission. They should give vague answers to strangers who call them, and reveal information to others on a need-to-know basis.

Everyone, whether they are a public figure or otherwise, should be wary of identity theft. It is not a good idea for anyone to fill out personal details on web forms. Survey sites, giveaways, competitions and even directories and social registers are a gold mine for people who are looking to collect personal information. Where a social register must be completed, try to opt-out of having the information shared. In other cases, do not volunteer information at all.

The principal should set up signal systems with friends and family members. These should include code words to inform each other that they are in danger, or that they should not go to a specific place. Anyone who could reasonably expect to be in danger should be taught to refuse to meet with unknown parties, especially at an unknown location and at a time of the stranger's choosing.

It is a good idea for both the executive and his family to share their schedules with each other so that everyone knows where the others will be and when they can expect to be home. There should be some agreements in place for what to do and who to contact if someone is out of touch for longer than agreed, of if they are late arriving to a scheduled appointment.

Executives should get into the habit of using neutral backgrounds for photographs that are sent out with press releases. Photographs that show them at home or at work are friendly and engaging but they can often reveal more about the person's whereabouts than expected. The executive and those who work with him should be encouraged to use a clean desk policy, so that there is no personal information left lying around for an intruder to look through after office hours.

In addition to keeping papers locked away, it should be company policy to lock and encrypt electronic devices. Laptops and desktops should store data on an encrypted drive, and phones should be set to auto-lock after a short period of time. Ideally, the devices should be connected to a corporate data system, which allows them to be wiped remotely should they be lost or stolen. Discourage the use of personal devices that do not support this.

Make sure that the executive is using a secure password for all of their services, including email, banking, cloud storage, social media and travel websites. They should not re-use passwords across sites, and they should change the passwords regularly.

SECURITY OUTSIDE THE HOME

Ideally, you would be with the principal at all times, and you would be able to perform reconnaissance on every journey that the principal makes before they make it. Unfortunately, this is not always possible. Sometimes the principal may need to make a journey without you. In fact, if you are protecting an executive it may be that you are only with them when they are making public appearances or travelling abroad. Mundane, day-to-day journeys may be made alone or with a chauffeur.

For those journeys, it is important that good preventative strategies are followed - the fewer people that know about the journey plans, the better. Ideally, the journey should be made in a non-descript vehicle – one that is fairly common in the area where the journey will be taking place.

The driver should be educated to never embark on a journey if the car has less than half a tank of fuel remaining. If anything looks out of place, the driver should detour as early as possible, keeping space on all sides of the car if there is the option to do so, and being mindful of their surroundings.

If an attack does take place, the principal should not leave the car unless remaining inside the car would put them in greater danger than getting out. The car can be used as a shield, and as a method of evasive action, assuming the driver knows how to do this. Bodyguards should be trained in evasive and defensive driving, and it is a good idea to ensure that any regular chauffeurs have similar training.

When the principal is being driven by a bodyguard or by a chauffeur, they should sit in the front passenger seat of the vehicle, and they should try not to draw attention to themselves. It is a good idea for them to observe their surroundings. They should not read or use a tablet device if possible.

If the principal is driving alone, they should inspect the car before entering it. They should pay particular attention to the exhaust (is it free from obstruction?), the tires (are they damaged), and the doors and windows. They should look inside the car to make sure that there is no evidence of forced entry and that there is no-one hiding in the back seat. Any car that the principal uses regularly should be kept clutter-free, so that if any strange objects are placed in the vehicle they will be easy to spot.

TRAVEL AND EVENT SECURITY

Depending on the level of protection that the principal requires, they may have a one-man protection "team" or they may have several people in charge of their safety. Very high profile people, such as members of the government or royal family may have between 30 or even 70 people in charge of keeping them safe.

Most bodyguards tend to work smaller jobs, but when taking care of celebrities or high profile executives who are making public appearances you may end up in a position where you have to work as a part of a team. As the personal bodyguard you are one of the most important people on the team, but the others have highly specialized and crucial roles to play.

Other members of a protection team include any social media or public relations people who field requests to see the principal, the driver who will be in charge of getting them to their destination, medical staff, mechanics, venue security staff, local law enforcement, the security advance team, personal escorts, and a team leader who co-ordinates the communication and the work of all of those people.

When deciding what size of team to employ, the first thing that the team leader will do will assess the level and the nature of the threats that have been brought to their attention. The importance of the principal will also be considered, as well as their preferences, personal circumstances and lifestyle. Depending on who the principal is, their job, and where they are travelling to, it may not be socially or politically acceptable for them to have a large entourage of visible bodyguards.

These circumstances must then be considered against the objectives of the protection team. There may be some compromises required to ensure the best possible resolution. Naturally, physical safety is paramount, but the team will also be concerned about mundane issues such as cost and manpower, as well as ensuring that the journey, meeting or public appearance goes as well as possible. They may also need to worry about the media and public opinion.

Planning and Operations

Before a major event there will be a planning phase. This is the chance for the bodyguard team to gather information, put in place any advance security and prepare any logistics that they will require. After this is done, the operations room will begin work on co-coordinating communications, briefing everyone involved (not just the protection team but also the principal and key associates), and arranging any equipment or services needed or the event.

The personal bodyguard is the one who will work closest with the principal. However, for a full circle of protection to be offered to the principal, there are several things that must be done and it is not always possible for a single bodyguard to offer them.

The bodyguard will use their observation skills to assess the safety of the principal at all times while they are with them, and to respond to any threats or potential threats in an efficient, safe and timely manner. If a bodyguard is doing their job well then they will respond to a lot of threats and changes in the environment without the principal becoming concerned or stressed about the scenarios that they were protected from.

Should the situation escalate beyond a certain point, then the bodyguard may even offer physical protection by acting as a personal shield for them. At its most obvious, this would be stepping in front of a projectile or intercepting a punch, but it can happen on a smaller scale, with the bodyguard creating space to save the principal from being jostled in a crowd.

The bodyguard should help the principal by providing end-to-end protection that is visible enough to deter anyone who has a malicious interest in the principal, but discreet enough that it protects the principal's public image. They should help the principal to avoid unsafe behaviors and routines, but still allow the principal to get on with their day-to-day lives.

Bodyguards may sometimes have to deal with officials, members of the public, or members of the principal's social circle. When doing this, they must be both diplomatic and assertive. The safety of the principal should come first at all times, but this does not mean that the principal's life or work can be put on hold for their protection. The bodyguard is in charge of safety, but they are still an employee of the principal.

In matters of operational security, the bodyguard will have to liaise with the rest of the protection team. They will need to lay out rules regarding the use of electronic communications, for example, and they will have to have plans in place for day-to-day administration, both within their own team and for travel, accommodation and scheduling for the principal and his associates.

During longer assignments – such as a diplomatic tour, it may become necessary for those involved with the protection of the principal to drill and practice while on assignment. If team members are rotated out at any point (for example if the principal is travelling and gets a new medical team in each country) then the team will need to work together to integrate those new members as quickly as possible and ensure operational continuity.

On long assignments, operatives can sometimes become tired or fatigued. It is essential that they take the time to take care of themselves and to ensure that they are physically and mentally fit. If they are ever not up to the job then they must ensure that alternative temporary cover is found.

TOOLS OF THE TRADE

A protection job follows a clear sequence. The bodyguard is informed of their task, and then they will use the following procedure:

- Perform a threat assessment

- Complete an initial liaison

- Perform an initial advance

- Appreciate the threat and situation

- Issue a warning order

- Issue an operation order

- Recon

- Complete the final liaison

- Carry out the operation

During this process they will rely on equipment ranging from communication tools to weapons (if such items are legal in the country where the operation is happening), medical equipment, firearms, surveillance equipment, security barriers, armor and vehicles.

The bodyguard and his team should have plans in place both for a safe operation, how to handle escalations, and how to handle the worst-case scenarios. Contingencies should exist for what to do if the principal is killed or injured, if one of the protection team is killed or injured, if the principal becomes trapped in a hostile environment, or if a vehicle is immobilized while the principal is using it.

In the event that the principal is injured, the job of the bodyguard is not over – they should find a way to get treatment for the principal while also ensuring their continued protection. The same is true if one of the team is injured. There should be a plan that will ensure that the team member gets medical aid while the majority of the team continues with the job of protecting the principal.

The bodyguard's job is to limit access to, and reduce the vulnerability of the principal while interfering as little as possible with their day-to-day routine. This can be best done if the principal is co-operative, as described earlier, and if a lot of research is done in advance. The more that is known about their medical history, behaviors, preferences and habits, the better.

A successful body guarding operation requires:

- The co-operation of the principal

- An accurate assessment of any threats

- Good planning by the protection team

- The correct deployment of resources

- The best possible use of those resources

Once the operation begins, the team will nominate a leader. Sometimes, in particular in scenarios where the team is a large one, the team leader is someone who will operate from a head office, relaying commands to other team members. In other scenarios, however, the team leader is the personal bodyguard.

The personal bodyguard operates at the centre of the circle of protection and will use both verbal commands and physical effort in order to ensure the safety of the principal at all times. He will not allow unknown persons to come into contact with the principal unless the contact has been pre-agreed and the person in question has been vetted. He should establish a good working relationship with the principal and any close associates because this will make the job easier.

Developing this rapport is one of the most important parts of being a bodyguard and it is something that a lot of would-be bodyguards fail to consider. A successful bodyguard is one who has the ability to blend in to almost any social and work circle. Bodyguards may be dealing with elderly politicians one week, child stars the next, and eccentric executives later in the year. Learning how to get all of those people on your side so that they work well with you is an essential skill.

In smaller teams, the bodyguard may simply act as a deterrent, travelling with the principal and ensuring their general safety against a low level, poorly defined threat. Their job should simply be to accompany the principal and stay out of their way as much as possible, while remaining alert for the possibility that a threat really does exist. These jobs can be boring, but it is important that they are taken seriously, because if a threat does surface rapid reactions are a must.

Bodyguards are placed in a difficult position in jobs like this. They will be spending a lot of time with their principal, and it is important that they put the principal at ease, but at the same time they must not be overly familiar. They should know when to speak, and when to stay quiet. They may be pulled into conversations that are not the sort of thing they would expect to speak about, and they should know when to answer, and when to stay quiet. If they do answer, they should know how much information to volunteer and who to speak to.

Bodyguards should err on the side of remaining silent when they are unsure what to do. A bodyguard that speaks too much is one that is unlikely to get re-hired. A bodyguard that is quiet and inconspicuous is one that most people would prefer to deal with.

Personal Escorts

In cases where a threat is clearly defined and has been assessed as being very serious, it may be wise to hire a personal escort. These escorts work with the main bodyguard to protect people against kidnapping or assassination attempts that have been deemed to be imminent or serious. Their job is both to act as a visible deterrent and a personal barrier. They will be expected to move in formation and to give body cover. They will also be expected to respond coherently and as a part of a team.

Personal escorts have a lower level of interaction with the principal than single bodyguards. Where a bodyguard may be with the principal at all times, the personal escort service may only be around while the bodyguard is travelling to public appearances. They will, once the principal has arrived at the venue (assuming the venue has been assessed by an advance team) step to one side and let the principal do their job, before returning later once the principal is ready to travel again.

ATTIRE AND BEHAVIOR

Both the bodyguard and the personal escort team must make an effort to dress appropriately and to blend in to the environment in which they are working. At a minimum, clothing should be suitable for the task at hand and the environment they will be in (so attire for a formal dinner would be different to that for a casual shopping trip), and the attire should be conservative enough to not draw attention to the bodyguard.

The principal's clothing preferences should be taken into account and the clothing should allow the bodyguard or the escort team to move freely so that they can perform their job. The clothes should be clean at all times.

The bodyguard should not smoke, drink alcohol, or engage in any unseemly or anti-social behaviors. This applies even if the principal themselves indulges in any such behaviors. The behavior of a bodyguard reflects on the personal protection team as much as it reflects on the principal, and indulging in anti-social behaviors, or partaking of certain substances could adversely affect the bodyguard's chances of being hired by another person at a later date.

Personal hygiene is something that the bodyguard and the rest of the team should take seriously. At a minimum, the bodyguard should be clean and well-shaven at all times, and wear clean and well-pressed clothing. However, beyond this the bodyguard should make an effort to use deodorants that do not have a strong scent, and they should avoid the use of cologne.

The bodyguard should always be prepared for the unexpected, and should have a small bag with them that contains a change of shirt, underwear, socks, and a tie, as well as a sewing kit, and some essential toiletries. This will serve as an overnight bag and ensure that the bodyguard is always presentable even if they are caught out overnight and then required to make a public appearance.

It is a good idea to carry a phone charger and a spare battery in that bag, and to keep a notepad and a pencil on hand as well. While the idea of a notepad and pencil may seem archaic today, it is important that you are not overly reliant on technology. Phone batteries can go flat and computer software can crash. A pencil and a piece of paper are far more reliable.

When it comes to interpersonal behaviors, a bodyguard should remember that they are always working. Sometimes, that work may put you in situations where there are temptations, but you must resist them. The principal may be enjoying a party, and may even encourage you to enjoy it with them. It is your job and responsibility to remain personable while reminding the principal that you cannot indulge because you must remain alert.

If you are dealing with people from many different cultures, then you will need to learn their cultures, and in particular their etiquette, so that you do not unwittingly commit a serious faux pas. Middle Eastern and Asian cultures have rules that are very different from the rules of the west, and it is easy to offend someone seriously with a few words or gestures that someone from the west would think nothing of.

Again, if in doubt it is best to err on the side of politeness and subservience. Ask questions of the operations team or the principal if you are not sure how to deal with a delegate or another executive.

UNARMED COMBAT

Unarmed combat is something that a lot of people expect to feature heavily in the role of a bodyguard, but this is not really the case. In most cases, the work that a bodyguard does involves reconnaissance, research, and observation. They help the principal avoid situations far more often than they extricate them from such situations.

Even so, every bodyguard should have experience with unarmed combat, and they should hone their skills on a regular basis. There are a lot of companies that teach close-quarters combat skills, including knife defense, weapon disarms, and joint manipulations. While some of these skills are interesting to know, they can create a false sense of confidence. The best training for someone who wants to be proficient in unarmed combat is training that is more pragmatic in its approach.

A diligent, fit and young person can get a basic grounding in boxing or Thai boxing with six months or so of regular training. They could add to that some training in Judo or wrestling to learn throws, takedowns, additional clinch work and how to fall safely. Submission grappling or Brazilian Jiu Jitsu are good choices for choke-holds and joint locks that can subdue an attacker while causing minimal harm – something that is incredibly important when you are considering working in the civilian arena.

Notice that traditional martial arts do not feature heavily in this list. The reason for that is that they do not usually involve practicing in a real fashion against a resisting opponent. Rather, they involve static training against a compliant opponent. This is not ideal because it creates the impression that the practitioner is proficient in a large number of techniques, when in fact they have never performed any of those techniques under pressure.

Practicing boxing, wrestling, judo or grappling involves "live" sparring where the trainees are trying to execute techniques against each other while the person they are training with is fighting back or resisting. Some critics say that these sports have rule sets – you are not going to be bitten while boxing, or punched while practicing Brazilian Jiu Jitsu. While this is true, their sparring is still the closest you can get to a real fight without actually fighting, and it allows you to pressure test your skills in a safe fashion.

Remember that if you are losing in a wrestling match, or being submitted in Brazilian Jiu Jitsu, this means that the opponent has control over you. It is unlikely that having the option to bite, eye-gouge or groin attack the opponent would turn the tide of the fight – after all, they are in a superior position, and they have the option to do the same thing to you.

Learning unarmed combat arts gives you a realistic idea of your abilities, and will allow you to assess what to do in situations where your safety and the safety of your principal are under threat. It will also give you the experience you need to speak confidently to the principal about things like self-defense training.

It is all too common for people who hire bodyguards to also go on self-defense courses and then get an unrealistic idea of their ability to take care of themselves. It is not possible to learn to effectively defend yourself in a short period of time, and these courses teach moves that are not guaranteed to work even when performed correctly, then fail to drill the moves often enough to ensure that they become ingrained in the principal's muscle memory.

Anyone who is likely to be exposed to physical threats should, at a minimum, have some training in breakfalls, the clinch, and how to escape from disadvantageous positions on the ground, as well as basic ways to subdue someone who is resisting. They do not necessarily need to be a good fighter, but those basic skills should be taught to them and practiced on a regular basis. The more exposure to dangerous situations the person will have, the more practice they should get.

As a bodyguard dealing directly with threats to someone's safety, you should train in restraint and control. The liability issues associated with striking someone and causing lasting damage are serious and should not be ignored. It is safer to pin someone than it is to punch them and risk concussion, or risk that when they fall to the ground after being knocked out they hit their head and suffer an even more serious injury.

Once you have your training, you must keep drilling the moves that you have learned, and you must take care of your physical fitness. The adrenaline dump associated with being in actual danger is hard to replicate in the gym (but competing in martial arts contests can replicate the feeling, to an extent) and you may get tired more quickly than you expect. The better your training and the fitter you are the better equipped you will be to serve your customers.

While this has focused on hand-to-hand combat, the same applies with weapons, but to an even greater degree. If you are a civilian considering entering the bodyguard industry you should think carefully before using weapons. A knife in the hands of someone who does not know how to use it or is not actually willing to use it is a liability because it may get turned against them.

A gun in the hands of someone who is not a skilled shooter is next to worthless. While a bullet can kill, a bullet that is in a gun that is sealed away in a hard to reach place is of no help when an emergency strikes. If you cannot draw, aim and fire the gun rapidly and accurately while under pressure you may as well not have it. If you are not completely confident in your knowledge of the law in your area and when it is legally appropriate to use the gun, you may as well not have it.

CONCLUSION

As you can see, bodyguards have a lot to think about. If you want to be successful in the bodyguard world you need to have skills both as a service provider, a liaison, an intelligence gatherer and a physical defense provider. It takes many years to develop these skills and the job is a hard one.

You should not enter the bodyguard industry if your main motivation for doing so is to meet celebrities or enjoy exposure to a glamorous lifestyle. Bodyguards work very hard, and they work long hours. The task can sometimes be a thankless one. Granted, it is often rewarding, but that is not always the case. Many principals do not understand the work that bodyguards do, and they are reluctant to cooperate.

As a bodyguard, your job is to keep someone safe, whether they want it or not. A bodyguard is only considered successful until they slip up, and if they make a mistake it could end their career for good.

If you understand what you are getting into by working in the close protection industry, and you still want to do so, then you should take a moment to find out about the opportunities that are available in your area for close protection officers, and network with existing workers. You may want to spend some time working as a personal escort in a team, while you get the training that you need to start your own business.

Spend some time learning about technology, the law, weapons and martial arts. Learn about different cultures and etiquette. Get as broad of a base of knowledge as you can so that you are not left floundering when your first assignment comes along. Practice communication skills, learn some words in a foreign language, and learn to read body language. You may not think that these skills will apply to your work but a versatile and well educated body guard will be more successful and more likely to get re-hired than one that is able to do little other than stand around and look intimidating.

Networking is another valuable skill for bodyguards. You may get some assignments through an agency, but if you are a trusted escort or protection provider for one businessman he may refer you to his friends and colleagues, and this will be an opportunity for you to grow your business so that you are no longer forced to rely on agencies for work. That is where you will have the chance to get the best employment opportunities and to start to make real money from your business. The financial reward, combined with the opportunity to make a difference and protect the wellbeing of public figures as well as their family members, is what makes so many people love the industry.

www.ingramcontent.com/pod-product-compliance
Lightning Source LLC
Chambersburg PA
CBHW072313200526
45168CB00014B/1432